Published by Chris Weston Publishing Ltd.
21 Great Sutton Street, London, EC1V ODY

Tel: +44(0) 207 566 9910
Fax: +44(0) 207 490 1723

Commissioning editor: Peter Moore
Editor: Daska Davis
Art Director: Mark Brewster
Production Director: Emma Goode

ISBN 978-0-9554595-0-4
Printed in Italy by Union Printing S.p.A.

At the heart of the image

CHRIS WESTON
WILDLIFE THROUGH A
NIKON LENS

Revealing the secrets of professional wildlife photography

There's only one way to do anything.
And that's the very best way you can.

George Weston

Contents

About the author

When I was fifteen years old I lived in Boston. Unfortunately for me, this Boston wasn't the colourful, vibrant city in the New England state of Massachusetts, rather the quiet market town in the English county of Lincolnshire, historically tied to its American namesake but a place best known for its Dutch-like landscape and the agricultural prowess of its inhabitants. What I am trying to say is that I grew up in a part of England that required much of one's imagination.

At school one day I was asked to select my preferred employer for a two-week work placement. The options weren't good. Potato planting, bulb cleaning or strawberry picking were three of the more attractive alternatives, as I recall. Seeing my inner turmoil, in a way only Dads can, my father asked me what I wanted to do for a career. With little hesitation I replied, "I want to be a photojournalist".

From where exactly that statement came, I can honestly say I have no idea. Not a clue. I mean, I remember wanting to be (at various times and in no particular order) a fireman, a policeman, a jet pilot, a train driver, a ski jumper and, of all things, an accountant. But, a photojournalist, well that was a new one even for me. Even so, at my father's behest and with the blessing of a somewhat perplexed school, at the tender age of fifteen I began my first ever assignment - and for another decade and a half at least, my last. You see, in between and like Dick Whittington before me, I became waylaid by London's promise of gold.

Nevertheless whatever ignited that school-time outburst of innocent, misguided aspiration, a seed had been sewn. And, sixteen years later, at the age of thirty-one, I realised that when I grew up I did indeed want to be a photojournalist. Today, I am the author of sixteen books - this is number seventeen. My work appears regularly in the photographic press and has been used in several ad campaigns at home and abroad. I lecture in photography and lead photographic workshops and tours both for my own company and others. But most of all, I am passionate about my work. There is a wide world out there and many stories still to be told. I hope I continue to tell them in the very best way I can.

Chris Weston

Introduction

For me, there is something remarkable about the ability of a single photograph to convey the circumstances and emotions associated with an entire event and, in cases, compel people to act. Over the years there have been some outstanding examples. I recall, for instance, Nick Ut's haunting black and white photograph of the nine-year-old Vietnamese girl, Kim Phuc, running naked along a road in agony from the Napalm that ate at her young body, and which, in 1972, brought to the attention of the world the true horrors of the Vietnamese war and helped to turn against the war the tide of public opinion. More recently there is Richard Drew's iconic and controversial photograph of the falling man, taken as the events and horrors of 9/11 unfolded.

Of course, none of the images in this book will win a Pulitzer - they were never intended to. For the most part this is a book about photographic technique, camera equipment and wildlife. At the same time, it is a book about so much more. The vision for the Through a Nikon Lens series derived from a desire to showcase superlative images and to reveal the equipment and techniques that made them possible. And, for this particular title in the series, I wanted to share not so much my personal view of wildlife and habitat, rather to provide a glimpse into our natural world from the animals' perspectives.

The images compiled here were shot over a six-year period from 2001 to 2006. They were captured using a range of equipment, from the pro-sumer F90X film camera to the latest in professional specification digital technology, and often utilising equipment and techniques rarely written about in books. The habitat I endured ranged from sub-Arctic wilderness to tropical rainforest and practically everything in between, across four continents - North America, Europe, Africa and Asia.

The species subjects cover a veritable who's who of the animal kingdom - from some of our closest living relatives, to our most dangerous competitors; our literary enemies to species we have driven to the edge of extinction. There is the strange and bizarre, the

Introduction

funny and furry. And, whatever the species, they all share a common attribute: they all have a story to tell. As the photographer for the project, my job was to tell it in the very best way I could.

Of course, that often meant going way further than simply turning up. For example, while photographing wild orang utan in the dense tropical rainforests of Borneo, I spent the best part of a week soaked in sweat, dangling from a rope 200 feet above the ground before I even managed a sighting worthy of a shot. It was uncomfortable and frustrating, but that is the life of a wildlife photographer. On another occasion, while trekking in the Parc National des Volcanes in Rwanda to photograph gorillas, it was so wet that by the time I returned to camp I had an inch of rain in the bottom of each boot. Whoever said this was a glamorous job?

For other images it was less the habitat and climate that proved the most challenging aspects of the shoot, more the equipment and technique needed to capture the moment. For example, to photograph the wide-angle perspective of the crocodile on page 96 - without doubt, one of Africa's most dangerous creatures - I had tried several techniques to get close safely, all without success. In the end I reverted to technology, some high tech some improvised, and hung the camera upside down on a monopod while holding it at arms length from the back of a 4x4, firing the shutter remotely via a laptop computer connection - the wonders of the digital age.

Environment and technology aside, the truth is that often the most challenging aspect of any assignment is the necessary research that takes place before even stepping foot in a plane, train or automobile. An aspect key to the success of this project (and of wildlife photography in general) was the ability to read and interpret animals' body language in order to predict behaviour. That meant many nights (and days) spent reading copious research documents and literature about the signs and signals that all animals give. Perhaps more importantly, it also meant finding field biologists and experts who would be prepared to share their knowledge and donate their time to the project. For certain the most time consuming part of my job involves sitting in front of a computer, typing search strings into Google and dialling telephone numbers that typically begin with 00 …

But, enough about me, for this book is really about the animal characters within it. When compiling the images to be used in the book I chose those photographs that most closely captured aspects of the subjects' personalities and behavioural traits. For example, one of my personal favourites is the image of the orang utan mother and baby on page 58. Anyone who has researched orang utan for any length of time will tell you that the babies need love almost as much as they need food and water; that the bond between mother and baby is one of the most intense in the natural world. And, for me, this intensity is overtly apparent within the composition. In this sense, this is a photograph where the camera openly and deliberately points just one-way. Equally, when photographing the wildebeeste migration in the Serengeti my principal subject was not the animals themselves, instead it was the very essence of what the migration is all about - movement.

And herein lies the true nature of this book. For while it is a book about photographic technique, camera equipment and wildlife, it is also about what compels us to pick up a camera at all. It is about the hidden depths of the photographic art and its ability to interpret visually the deeper meanings of the natural world. It is about communication and communicating, it is about love and laughter, it is about movement and camouflage and action and reaction. It is about all those things that together form life. And all captured through a Nikon lens.

Light & exposure

Light and exposure are photographers' most influential visual tools.

A subtle shift of the delicate balance between shutter speed and lens aperture, or a tweaking of metering mode can transform quickly and effectively the visual impact our photographs make, at once turning the ordinary into the extraordinary. In itself it is perhaps the single, most powerful weapon in our overflowing kitbags.

The technical aspects of exposure are well documented, and once these have been understood and we have become proficient in their use, it is how we apply them in the field that is the true test of our photographic skill. For while a camera's automated exposure system often will produce an acceptable result when left to its own devices, its vacuous nature will produce compelling images infrequently, and then more by luck than judgement.

Judgement is the photographer's job. As we stand behind our cameras, framing a tiny portion of the world within the confines of our viewfinders, we must consider the visual statement we are attempting to make and use the tools at our disposal to define them in photographic form. In this sense, as the great American photographer, Freeman Patterson, once said, the camera points both ways. That's to say, the images the camera records are a direct reflection on the judgements we make.

As a professional photographer I see it as my responsibility to develop not just my own skills and business, but also the level of image making in the industry as a whole. When confronted by a scene or subject to photograph I ask myself the question, "How can I shoot this differently?" Often the answer lies in altering the camera's view of exposure to that of my own.

Take for example the deeply atmospheric image of a herd of elephants marching towards the Chobe River in Botswana at the break of day (page 17). Had I accepted the camera's automatic exposure assessment I would have lost the powerful graphic statement made by the silhouetted pachyerms, the bold and vivid colour of the sky, and the magical rays of light that punctuate the dusty landscape. Instead I made a judgement on how I wanted to portray this scene and took the appropriate exposure decisions accordingly. The resulting image is very different to the one the camera would have recorded before my intervention.

It is easy to become caught up in the pursuit of the 'perfect' exposure. In reality no such thing exists. Who is to say, for example, that my exposure setting for the photograph of the elephants in Chobe National Park is any more correct than that which the camera chose automatically? Instead of pursuing a technical holy grail our aim should be to record faithful exposures; exposures that create an image of the subject or scene as we see it in our hearts and minds, subject to all our life experiences, prejudices and emotions.

This first section of the book is dedicated to those images that rely on the subtleties of exposure to achieve their visual goal. In each it is the careful manipulation of light that gives the images their meaning, creating powerful graphic statements that inform our minds and invade our conscience.

Mountain gorilla, Parc National des Volcanes, Rwanda
Light is the essential building block of photography. Exposure is the tool we use to turn those building blocks into photographic design.

◄ IN THE BAG

Camera:	**D200**
Lens:	**70-200mm f/2.8 AF-S VR**
Focal length:	**200mm**
Metering mode:	**Matrix**
Exposure mode:	**Aperture-priority auto**
Shutter speed:	**1/45**
Lens aperture:	**F/2.8**

Into the light

The following series of images were all taken photographing into the light. Exposure has been controlled to create a silhouette of the subject, typically by metering the highlights and allowing the shadow areas to under-expose. The technique is relatively simple. Even so, even slight adjustments and tweaks to exposure settings can have far reaching consequences. For example, compare the two images of elephants on pages 17 and 18. These were taken moments apart and yet, by slightly under-exposing the highlights in the landscape-format image (page 17) the colour of the sky has been greatly affected. Of the two I prefer the image on page 17 but the photograph on page 18 is closer to reality.

African elephants, Chobe National Park, Botswana

IN THE BAG ▶

Camera:	**D2X**
Lens:	**70-200mm f/2.8 AF-S VR with TC 20-E**
Focal length:	**400mm**
Metering mode:	**Spot**
Exposure mode:	**Aperture-priority auto**
Shutter speed:	**1/640**
Lens aperture:	**F/7.1**

Into the light

**African elephants,
Chobe National Park, Botswana**

IN THE BAG ▶

Camera:	**D2X**
Lens:	**70-200mm f/2.8 AF-S with TC 20-E**
Focal length:	**320mm**
Metering mode:	**Spot**
Exposure mode:	**Aperture-priority auto**
Shutter speed:	**1/250**
Lens aperture:	**F/7.1**

Silhouettes make powerful graphic statements. I find giraffe difficult subjects to photograph - they simply aren't designed for your average camera viewfinder! However, by thinking of the subject in terms of design elements, as opposed to a wildlife subject, I finally achieved a shot I am proud of.

The same principal has been applied to the composition of the image of vultures resting on a tree (overleaf). As an aside, consider how the use of colour has influenced your emotional response to these two images. The warm glow of the orange sunset gives the image of the giraffe a tranquil ambience, while the cold blue sky behind the vultures enhances the stark dagger-like branches of the tree in a way that compliments the subject.

Giraffe, Kruger National Park, South Africa

IN THE BAG ▶

Camera:	**D100**
Lens:	**80-400mm f/4.5-5.6 AF VR**
Focal length:	**400mm**
Metering mode:	**Spot**
Exposure mode:	**Aperture-priority auto**
Shutter speed:	**1/640**
Lens aperture:	**F/5.6**

Malachite kingfisher, Kruger National Park, South Africa.
Golden light from a setting sun reflects off surface water to provide an ideal background to the silhouette.

◀ IN THE BAG

Camera:	**D2X**
Lens:	**600mm f/4 AF**
Focal length:	**600mm**
Metering mode:	**Spot**
Exposure mode:	**Aperture-priority auto**
Shutter speed:	**1/350**
Lens aperture:	**F/8**

Vultures, Kruger National Park, South Africa

◀ IN THE BAG

Camera:	**D100**
Lens:	**70-200mm f/2.8 AF-S VR**
Focal length:	**70mm**
Metering mode:	**Matrix**
Exposure mode:	**Aperture-priority auto**
Shutter speed:	**1/3000**
Lens aperture:	**F/8**

Into the light

African elephant, Greater Kruger National Park, South Africa
As dawn breaks a young elephant marches around a waterhole, silhouetted against the pink and blue sky.

◄ IN THE BAG

Camera:	**D100**
Lens:	**24-120 f/3.5-5.6 AF**
Focal length:	**66mm**
Metering mode:	**Matrix**
Exposure mode:	**Aperture-priority auto**
Shutter speed:	**1/1000**
Lens aperture:	**F/5.6**

Brown bear, Katmai National Park, Alaska, USA
Late in the day the low angle of the never-setting sun highlights the bushy Alaskan wilderness. Seemingly, this is one bear ready for bed.

IN THE BAG ►

Camera:	**D2X**
Lens:	**80-400mm f/4.5-5.6 AF VR**
Focal length:	**400mm**
Metering mode:	**Spot**
Exposure mode:	**Aperture-priority auto**
Shutter speed:	**1/250**
Lens aperture:	**F/8**

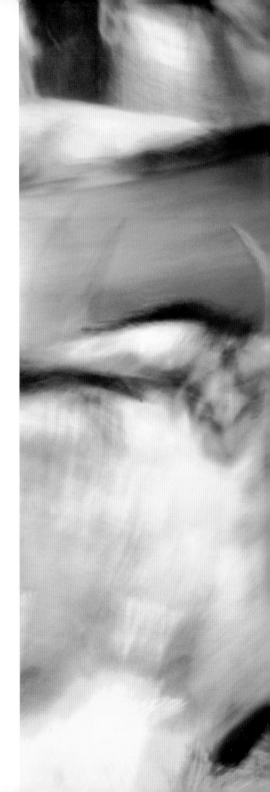

The aesthetic effects of blur

There was a time when the golden rule of wildlife photography was to set a fast shutter speed to freeze the appearance of motion. Thankfully we've moved on.

I first noticed long-time exposure shots of wildlife in the National Geographic, where photographers such as Michael 'Nick' Nichols and Joel Sartore are great exponents of the technique. The art of blurring movement to create the visual impression of speed and motion is in attaining the most effective shutter speed - too fast and the effect is lost, too slow and the image lacks sufficient definition. For all the following images I set a slow shutter speed to recreate visually the ambiance of the events I was photographing.

Wildebeeste, Serengeti National Park, Tanzania

IN THE BAG ▶

Camera:	**D2X**
Lens:	**70-200mm f/2.8 AF-S VR with TC 20-E**
Focal length:	**400mm**
Metering mode:	**Matrix**
Exposure mode:	**Aperture-priority auto**
Shutter speed:	**1/2**
Lens aperture:	**F/45**

Every year in Kenya and Tanzania over 1.5 million wildebeeste migrate between the Serengeti and Masai Mara. It is an amazing sight to behold - so many animals, so much movement. To capture a true sense of the scene, I selected different focal length lenses to alter the perspective in each and used shutter speeds ranging from 1/2 - 1/15 sec to blur motion. In each image the animals merge, as if a single being, much as they often appear to do in real life during the migration.

Wildebeeste, Serengeti National Park, Tanzania

IN THE BAG ▶

Camera:	**D2X**
Lens:	**70-200mm f/2.8 AF-S VR**
Focal length:	**200mm**
Metering mode:	**Matrix**
Exposure mode:	**Aperture-priority auto**
Shutter speed:	**1/10**
Lens aperture:	**F/22**

Wildebeeste, Serengeti National Park, Tanzania

◀ **IN THE BAG**

Camera:	**D2X**
Lens:	**70-200mm f/2.8 AF-S VR**
Focal length:	**200mm**
Metering mode:	**Matrix**
Exposure mode:	**Aperture-priority auto**
Shutter speed:	**1/15**
Lens aperture:	**F/22**

Being grazers, zebra are constantly on the move and I wanted to capture the essence of this aspect of their life. This image results from a combination of two techniques. First I set a slow shutter speed to blur the appearance of motion. Secondly it was shot from a moving jeep with the camera held simply by the strap. I fired the shutter with a remote cord. The combination of lateral and vertical movement has added an additional dimension to the photograph. The sepia tone was created later using Adobe Photoshop software.

Burchell's zebra, Ngorongoro Crater, Tanzania

IN THE BAG ▲

Camera:	**D2X**
Lens:	**70-200mm f/2.8 AF-S VR**
Focal length:	**130mm**
Metering mode:	**Matrix**
Exposure mode:	**Aperture-priority auto**
Shutter speed:	**1/10**
Lens aperture:	**F/22**

The aesthetic effects of blur

A couple of years ago I had the pleasure - if you can call it that - of spending a day with a pod of wallowing hippos in Mkuze National Park, in South Africa. The experience was not dissimilar to spending the same length of time in a boys' locker room. They burped, farted and snorted; they bumped, banged and fought. Hippos, it seems, are lacking in manners and social etiquette. Once again, a slow shutter speed has helped to recreate the emotion of the scene as I saw it.

Hippopotamus, Mkuze National Park, South Africa

◀ **IN THE BAG**

Camera:	**F5**
Lens:	**300mm f/2.8 AF**
Focal length:	**300mm**
Metering mode:	**Matrix**
Exposure mode:	**Aperture-priority auto**
Shutter speed:	**1/20**
Lens aperture:	**F/11**

Black-winged stilt,
Mkuze National Park, South Africa
Perpetually on the move, the long legs of the stilt propel it along the edge of a pan in search of food.

◀ IN THE BAG

Camera:	**D100**
Lens:	**600mm f/4 AF**
Focal length:	**600mm**
Metering mode:	**Matrix**
Exposure mode:	**Aperture-priority auto**
Shutter speed:	**1/15**
Lens aperture:	**F/5.6**

Grey wolf, Kingussie, Scotland (captive)
Despite their fearsome reputation wolves in the wild are like ghosts, and are rarely seen by humans. A slow shutter speed has helped blend animal and environment, creating the appearance of an apparition. The sepia tone was created in Adobe Photoshop software.

IN THE BAG ▶

Camera:	**D2H**
Lens:	**80-400 f/4.5-5.6 AF VR**
Focal length:	**310mm**
Metering mode:	**Matrix**
Exposure mode:	**Aperture-priority auto**
Shutter speed:	**1/30**
Lens aperture:	**F/16**

Golden jackal, Ngorongoro Crater, Tanzania
What I noticed in this scene was not the jackal specifically but the beautiful colouring of the grasses in the background, which is emphasised by a combination of exposure technique (slow shutter speed) and camera technique (panning).

IN THE BAG ▶

Camera:	**D2X**
Lens:	**80-400mm f/4.5-5.6 AF VR**
Focal length:	**400mm**
Metering mode:	**Matrix**
Exposure mode:	**Aperture-priority auto**
Shutter speed:	**1/10**
Lens aperture:	**F/22**

Grey wolf, Minnesota, USA
No it's not a black Labrador! Wolves' pelage ranges from black to white, depending to some extent on habitat. I photographed this individual in dense woodland in Minnesota. In reality the environment was much darker than it appears in photographic form but the digital sensor has helped in securing the image. I particularly liked the kaleidoscopic effect of the colours in the background, picked out by the mottled light.

IN THE BAG ▲

Camera:	**D2H**
Lens:	**70-200mm f/2.8 AF-S VR**
Focal length:	**120mm**
Metering mode:	**Matrix**
Exposure mode:	**Aperture-priority auto**
Shutter speed:	**1/20**
Lens aperture:	**F/8**

It's just a matter of time

When sharpness is called for faster shutter speeds freeze the appearance of motion, capturing aspects of animal behaviour and detail that are otherwise lost.

Generally the shutter alone determines the length of exposure, but you also have another tool at your disposal - flash. A typical burst of flash lasts for around 1/10,000 sec and, where flash provides the principal illumination, its duration also becomes the effective shutter speed. When I photographed the fox (page 45) I used this flash technique to freeze the action of the animal leaping from the grassy mound in the water. The conditions were much darker than the photograph appears, the flash adding illumination to the foreground. For each of the subsequent images a fast shutter speed was chosen to reveal in detail events as they unfolded.

It's just a matter of time

With the D100 set to high-speed continuous frame advance, a burst of images has captured this yearling brown bear as it hunts for salmon in Brooks River in Alaska's Katmai National Park. Bears use many different techniques for catching salmon but this is a favourite of the younger bears, which haven't the experience to consider less energy-consuming methods. Either that or they simply enjoy the chase, which, I suspect, is their real motivation.

Brown bear yearling, Katmai National Park, Alaska, USA

◄▲► **IN THE BAG**

Camera:	**D100**
Lens:	**600mm f/4 AF**
Focal length:	**600mm**
Metering mode:	**Matrix**
Exposure mode:	**Aperture-priority auto**
Shutter speed:	**1/500**
Lens aperture:	**F/8**

Black-headed gull, Radipole Nature Reserve, Weymouth, UK

A burst of electronic flash has been used in combination with a relatively slow shutter speed to capture this emotive image of a black-headed gull in flight, taken at dusk. The flash has captured the fine detail of the feathers and eye, while the slow shutter speed adds a sense of movement in the bird's wings.

IN THE BAG ▶

Camera:	**D2X**
Lens:	**12-24mm AF**
Focal length:	**18mm**
Exposure mode:	**Aperture-priority**
Shutter speed:	**1/160**
Lens aperture:	**F/8**
Flash:	**SB-800**

It's just a matter of time

Burchell's zebra, Serengeti National Park, Tanzania
During the mating season stallions constantly vie for dominance over a territory and control over a hareem of females.

◄ **IN THE BAG**

Camera:	**D2X**
Lens:	**70-200mm f/2.8 AF-S VR with TC-20E**
Focal length:	**400mm**
Metering mode:	**Matrix**
Exposure mode:	**Aperture-priority**
Shutter speed:	**1/350**
Lens aperture:	**F/11**

Burchell's zebra, Serengeti National Park, Tanzania
Adult zebra are at their most vulnerable when drinking. This herd was spooked by the presence of a predator and a fast shutter speed has captured tumult and frenzy of the moment.

IN THE BAG ►

Camera:	**D2X**
Lens:	**600mm f/4 AF**
Focal length:	**600mm**
Metering mode:	**Matrix**
Exposure mode:	**Aperture-priority auto**
Shutter speed:	**1/1000**
Lens aperture:	**F/11**

It's just a matter of time

Gannet, Bass Rock, Scotland
Bass Rock is an excellent location for close up views of gannets. However, the shear number makes it difficult to isolate individuals, even in flight.

◀ **IN THE BAG**

Camera:	**D2X**
Lens:	**70-200mm F/2.8 AF-S VR**
Focal length:	**180mm**
Metering mode:	**Spot**
Exposure mode:	**Aperture-priority**
Shutter speed:	**1/8000**
Lens aperture:	**F/2.8**

Gannet, Bass Rock, Scotland
Territory is fiercely protected and gannets, when landing, face a gauntlet of sharp beaks that protect occupied space.

IN THE BAG ▶

Camera:	**D2X**
Lens:	**70-200mm f/2.8 AF-S VR**
Focal length:	**155mm**
Metering mode:	**Matrix**
Exposure mode:	**Aperture-priority**
Shutter speed:	**1/750**
Lens aperture:	**F/7.1**

It's just a matter of time

Nile Crocodile, Greater Kruger National Park, South Africa
Crocodiles move out of the water with alarming speed. A fast shutter speed has helped to capture the action.

◀ **IN THE BAG**

Camera:	**D200**
Lens:	**70-200mm f/2.8 AF-S VR**
Focal length:	**200mm**
Metering mode:	**Matrix**
Exposure mode:	**Aperture-priority**
Shutter speed:	**1/350**
Lens aperture:	**F/8**

Red fox, Minnesota, USA
A combination of high-power flash and a fast shutter speed has helped to freeze the action of this acrobatic fox.

IN THE BAG ▶

Camera:	**D2H**
Lens:	**12-24mmf/4 AF-S DX**
Focal length:	**24mm**
Metering mode:	**Matrix**
Exposure mode:	**Aperture-priority auto**
Shutter speed:	**1/2000**
Lens aperture:	**F/5.6**
Flash:	**SB-800 Speedlight**

It's just a matter of time

African leopard, Greater Kruger National Park, South Africa

Anticipation was the key to this shot of a leopard leaping up a tree - knowing how to frame the image in conjunction with the use of the predictive focus technique.

IN THE BAG ▶

Camera:	**D2X**
Lens:	**70-200mm f/2.8 AF-S VR**
Focal length:	**105mm**
Metering mode:	**Matrix**
Exposure mode:	**Aperture-priority**
Shutter speed:	**1/640**
Lens aperture:	**F/2.8**

African leopard, Greater Kruger National Park, South Africa
Coming down, however, the leopard moved with greater speed and camera panning along the vertical plane has helped to keep the subject sharp.

IN THE BAG ▶

Camera:	**D2H**
Lens:	**24-120mm f/3.5-5.6 AF-S VR**
Focal length:	**80mm**
Metering mode:	**Matrix**
Exposure mode:	**Aperture-priority auto**
Shutter speed:	**1/90**
Lens aperture:	**F/4.5**

Coyote, Minnesota, USA
Perhaps the hardest aspect of photographing wildlife in action is achieving the right balance between apparent-motion and retaining detail. Here I used a mid-range shutter speed of 1/60 to create a level of blur in the animals body while keeping the important parts of the coyote, its head and eye, relatively sharp.

IN THE BAG ▶

Camera:	**D100**
Lens:	**70-200mm f/2.8 AF-S VR**
Focal length:	**185mm**
Metering mode:	**Matrix**
Exposure mode:	**Aperture-priority auto**
Shutter speed:	**1/60**
Lens aperture:	**F/16**

Isolation
and a sense of place

An animal's relationship with its surroundings can be managed and controlled via exposure settings.

Lens aperture is one of three factors affecting depth-of-field - the larger the aperture the smaller the zone of apparent sharpness (depth of field). Compare the images of the golden jackal (page 50) and the Malachite kingfisher (page 51). In the former, by selecting a smaller aperture to increase depth of field, I have created a link between the jackal and the flamingos in the background. Both mammal and birds have a sense of place, and the photograph recreates visually the predator/prey relationship. When photographing the kingfisher my aim was to isolate it, placing all of the visual emphasis on the subject. A large aperture has minimized depth of field blurring the distracting background into a neutral plane of almost mono tone. Incidentally, the central positioning of the bird has added to its apparent isolation. So through exposure we can control the emphasis of an image and manipulate how the viewer sees the subjects within a scene.

Golden jackal and lesser flamingos, Ngorongoro Crater, Tanzania

◄ **IN THE BAG**

Camera:	**D100**
Lens:	**600mm f/4 AF**
Focal length:	**600mm**
Metering mode:	**Matrix**
Exposure mode:	**Aperture-priority auto**
Shutter speed:	**1/500**
Lens aperture:	**F/8**

Malachite kingfisher, Kruger National Park, South Africa

IN THE BAG ▲

Camera:	**D2X**
Lens:	**600mm f/4 AF**
Focal length:	**600mm**
Metering mode:	**Matrix**
Exposure mode:	**Aperture-priority auto**
Shutter speed:	**1/400**
Lens aperture:	**F/8**

Isolation and a sense of place

African leopard, Welwyn, UK (captive)
A very shallow depth of field has obscured the unnatural and distracting background of this leopard's enclosure. In so doing all the emphasis is placed on the charismatic face of the big cat.

◀ IN THE BAG

Camera:	**F90X**
Lens:	**80-200mm f/2.8 AF**
Focal length:	**200mm**
Metering mode:	**Matrix**
Exposure mode:	**Aperture-priority auto**
Shutter speed:	**1/250**
Lens aperture:	**F/4**

African lion cub, Kruger National Park, South Africa

◄ IN THE BAG

Camera:	**F5**
Lens:	**300mm f/2.8 AF**
Focal length:	**300mm**
Metering mode:	**Matrix**
Exposure mode:	**Aperture-priority auto**
Shutter speed:	**1/60**
Lens aperture:	**F/2.8**

Baboon with baby, Kruger National Park, South Africa

By framing this image to deliberately exclude important features (such as the eye) of the mother, I have placed the emphasis of the image on the baby. A central position has also helped to isolate, and further emphasise, within the frame the baby baboon.

◄ IN THE BAG

Camera:	**D200**
Lens:	**70-200mm f/2.8 AF-S VR**
Focal length:	**150mm**
Metering mode:	**Matrix**
Exposure mode:	**Aperture-priority**
Shutter speed:	**1/13**
Lens aperture:	**F/5.6**

Hippopotamuses, Kruger National Park, South Africa

The hippopotamus in the background is intrinsic to this image but of less importance than the two animals in the foreground. The trick with this shot was to manage depth of field so that the background hippo was discernable but not distracting.

IN THE BAG ▲

Camera:	**D2H**
Lens:	**300mm f/2.8 AF with TC 20-E**
Focal length:	**600mm**
Metering mode:	**Matrix**
Exposure mode:	**Aperture-priority auto**
Shutter speed:	**1/180**
Lens aperture:	**F/11**

Baboon, Kruger National Park, South Africa
It was the thoughtful look on this baboon's face that I wanted to capture, and so set a wide aperture to minimize depth of field.

◄ **IN THE BAG**

Camera:	**D100**
Lens:	**600mm f/4 AF**
Focal length:	**600mm**
Metering mode:	**Matrix**
Exposure mode:	**Aperture-priority auto**
Shutter speed:	**1/250**
Lens aperture:	**F/5.6**

Capture

Photography is a means of communication.

When we make an image what we are trying to do is to elicit from the viewer an emotional response, and to evoke thought. Our endeavour always should be to engender happiness, cheerfulness, elation, jubilation, contentment or even sadness. We should aim to make people laugh and cry, to wonder and adore. Perhaps too our photographs should stir people to question and contemplation, provoke action and incite flurry. How can all this be achieved with a two-dimensional image?

The camera provides us with the perfect tool - the viewfinder. Its confines provide us with a window on our world, a means of designating and framing a moment in time. Yet how many photographers truly observe through the viewfinder, rather than merely look at what they see? How often do you notice the details that make or break an image? For example, the catchlight that brings life to an otherwise soulless eye, or the fleeting moment of requited love shared between a mother and her young. Like listening, seeing is a skill that must be practiced and developed for our photographic ambitions to be rewarded. There is a simple test that I apply when photographing wildlife. I ask myself the question, "How would I caption this image?" If the only answer I can summon is the specie's name then I rarely press the shutter. Picture in your mind a photograph of a bird perched on a branch

with its beak closed. Now consider the same image taken an instant later with the beak open. Which is the stronger picture? In the former, the caption would read, Bird perched on branch. The latter caption, however, would add the verb singing, and the image would be better for it.

The photograph on page 58 is one of my personal favourites. Anyone who has studied orang utan will tell you that a baby orang utan needs to feel love almost as much as it needs nourishment. In this single image, taken in the briefest moment, the piquant emotion shared between mother and baby is captured with a power and poignancy that negates further description, and in an instant this belief is held to be true. It is moments like these on which we should exhaust our batteries and fill our memories.

Capturing the moment, knowing when is the right time to press the shutter is a skill that wildlife photographers develop over time and through their experiences in the field. It is not only a question of recognition but also one of anticipation and fulfilment. It is a prerequisite that to be successful a wildlife photographer must know how to operate the camera instinctively, without recourse to second thought. It is much like driving a car. Anyone who has been driving long enough no longer thinks about the process of driving. We don't get in

Capture

our cars and consciously consider handbrake off, clutch out, throttle down. We just do it. It is to the same degree of competency that you should know how to use your camera.

But perhaps even more important is knowledge of biology and animal behaviour. It is not enough to witness a wild event and then attempt to capture it on film or in pixels. I can guarantee that even the fastest draw in the west is too slow for most wildlife subjects. By the time your finger reacts to the message from your brain saying "press shutter now" the moment will almost certainly be over. Like the gunmen at a clay shoot your aim needs to be ahead of the target. And the information you need to foresee the composition is right there before you. All animals communicate to tell us what they are thinking. It's simply that few of us bother to learn their language. For those that do your efforts will be rewarded in the images you make.

The following series of images all fall within the category 'a moment in time'. They have been chosen as representative of a photograph's ultimate aim - to communicate. Although they are captioned, each in their own way is beyond need of words. Each has a message to convey and a story to tell. How their stories end … well, that's up to you.

Orang utan mother with baby, Sabah, Borneo
Knowing when is the moment to press the shutter is dependent on you understanding the true nature of your subject. For me, this image isn't a picture of orang utan, it is a visual study of parental love.

IN THE BAG ▶

Camera:	**D2X**
Lens:	**200-400mm f/4 AF-S VR**
Focal length:	**220mm**
Metering mode:	**Matrix**
Exposure mode:	**Aperture-priority**
Shutter speed:	**1/10**
Lens aperture:	**F/4**

The remarkable
behaviour
of animals

Photography has the power to reveal and inform.

Wildlife photographers are in a unique position to capture moments of animal behaviour that reveal aspects of the natural world that few people ever get to see in the wild. Take for example the image of the tiny lilac-breasted roller attacking the mighty Bateleur eagle, a real-life David versus Goliath. I almost missed the event myself and only saw it as I looked up and away from the wildebeeste migration to clear some dust from my eye. Luck or fate, I'll never know. Each of the pictures over the next few pages are captured moments of animals behaving naturally and in a way few have the opportunity to observe in life.

Yellow-billed oxpecker, Masai Mara National Reserve, Kenya

Animal behaviour can be learned from books but is learned quicker when experienced in the field, and this behavioural shot of oxpeckers is a good example of on-the-job training. I watched them from the jeep for some time and noticed these two birds continually squabbling over pecking rights. As I watched I memorized the pattern of their behaviour and chose my moment carefully. The timing was perfect.

◀ IN THE BAG

Camera:	**D100**
Lens:	**600mm f/4 AF**
Focal length:	**600mm**
Metering mode:	**Matrix**
Exposure mode:	**Aperture-priority auto**
Shutter speed:	**1/320**
Lens aperture:	**F/8**

African lion and lioness, Masai Mara National Reserve, Kenya

During mating male lions bite the scruff the lionesses neck to avoid being bitten when dismounting. Lions' penises are barbed and extraction can be painful!

IN THE BAG ▶

Camera:	**D100**
Lens:	**600mm F/4 AF**
Focal length:	**600mm**
Metering mode:	**Matrix**
Exposure mode:	**Aperture-priority auto**
Shutter speed:	**1/250**
Lens aperture:	**F/8**

The remarkable behaviour of animals

African lion and lioness,
Masai Mara National Reserve, Kenya
Image sequences can be used effectively to show aspects of animal behaviour. In the wild lions mate for several days at a time and continuously throughout the day. This pair was at it every seven minutes!

IN THE BAG ▲ ▶

Camera:	**D2X**
Lens:	**80-400mm f/4.5-5.6 AF VR**
Focal length:	**220mm**
Metering mode:	**Matrix**
Exposure mode:	**Aperture-priority auto**
Shutter speed:	**1/640**
Lens aperture:	**F/11**

Lion, Masai Mara National Reserve, Kenya
This image shows a typical behavioural trait of male lions
during mating.

◀ IN THE BAG

Camera:	**D2X**
Lens:	**70-200mm f/2.8 AF-S VR**
Focal length:	**200mm**
Metering mode:	**Matrix**
Exposure mode:	**Aperture-priority**
Shutter speed:	**1/250**
Lens aperture:	**F/5.6**

Wolf pack, Kingussie, Scotland (captive)
I have the RAF to thank for this shot of wolves during a
chorus howl. Every time a low-flying jet came within a
couple of miles the animals would display this behaviour.
Once the jets had flown past, the wolves returned to
foraging.

IN THE BAG ▶

Camera:	**D100**
Lens:	**600mm f/4 AF**
Focal length:	**600mm**
Metering mode:	**Matrix**
Exposure mode:	**Aperture-priority auto**
Shutter speed:	**1/640**
Lens aperture:	**F/5.6**

Coyotes, Minnesota, USA
Territorial animals often have to assert their dominance. Despite the apparent ferocity of this attack neither animal was harmed during the encounter.

◀ IN THE BAG

Camera:	**D2H**
Lens:	**70-200 f/2.8 AF-S VR**
Focal length:	**150mm**
Metering mode:	**Matrix**
Exposure mode:	**Aperture-priority auto**
Shutter speed:	**1/500**
Lens aperture:	**F/11**

Nile crocodile, Limpopo, South Africa
It is rare to see a crocodile making a kill. An unfortunate warthog wandered a little too close to the riverbank and pork belly was on the menu that day. A case of wrong time, wrong place.

IN THE BAG ▶

Camera:	**D2H**
Lens:	**24-120mm f/3.4-5.6 AF-S VR**
Focal length:	**120mm**
Metering mode:	**Matrix**
Exposure mode:	**Aperture-priority auto**
Shutter speed:	**1/400**
Lens aperture:	**F/8**

Brown bear, Katmai National Park, Alaska, USA
A little back lighting has highlighted the myriad droplets of water shaken from the bears fur. Fishing for salmon can get you wet … very wet. As can photographing bears!

◄ IN THE BAG

Camera:	**D2X**
Lens:	**600mm f/4 AF**
Focal length:	**600mm**
Metering mode:	**Matrix**
Exposure mode:	**Aperture-priority auto**
Shutter speed:	**1/750**
Lens aperture:	**F/5.6**

Eliciting an emotional response

Like a good story a compelling image has the power to awaken our emotions.

If the aim of photography is to elicit an emotional response then the following selection of images will be the proof of the pudding. Wildlife photographers tend to be emotive people and perhaps it is an essential attribute for a successful career. There is no doubt that having an affinity for your subject will show in the images you make. For example, I particularly like elephants and spend a lot of time photographing them. The image on page 70 was captured in Chobe National Park in 2005 and still makes me laugh today. I can imagine an endless number of captions for this particular scene. I wonder, how would you caption this image?

**African elephant,
Chobe National Park, Botswana**

◀ **IN THE BAG**

Camera:	**D2X**
Lens:	**70-200mm f/2.8 AF-S VR**
Focal length:	**200mm**
Metering mode:	**Matrix**
Exposure mode:	**Aperture-priority auto**
Shutter speed:	**1/90**
Lens aperture:	**F/8**

Indian elephants, Pinnawala Orphanage, Sri Lanka (captive)
Elephants are tactile creatures and enjoy one another's company. The close crop used to
make this image has emphasised the relationship between the two animals.

IN THE BAG ▲

Camera:	**F5**
Lens:	**24-120mm f/3.5-5.6 AF**
Focal length:	**120mm**
Metering mode:	**Matrix**
Exposure mode:	**Aperture-priority auto**
Shutter speed:	**1/250**
Lens aperture:	**F/5.6**

Brown bear, Katmai National Park, Alaska, USA

◀ **IN THE BAG**

Camera:	**D2X**
Lens:	**600mm f/4 AF**
Focal length:	**600mm**
Metering mode:	**Matrix**
Exposure mode:	**Aperture-priority**
Shutter speed:	**1/125**
Lens aperture:	**F/8**

Brown bear, Katmai National Park, Alaska, USA

Bears typically catch salmon along the Alaskan coast but this enterprising individual managed to snag himself a flounder. The only problem was he had no idea what to do with it!

IN THE BAG ▲

Camera:	**D2X**
Lens:	**600mm f/4 AF**
Focal length:	**600mm**
Metering mode:	**Matrix**
Exposure mode:	**Aperture-priority**
Shutter speed:	**1/125**
Lens aperture:	**F/8**

Wildebeeste, Ngorongoro Crater, Tanzania

Crash, bang, wallop, what a picture ... Wildebeeste are one of Nature's naturally amusing creatures and provide plenty of opportunity for pictures to make you smile. Here's another one where several possible captions spring to mind.

IN THE BAG ▶

Camera:	**D2X**
Lens:	**80-400mm f/4.5-5.6 AF**
Focal length:	**400mm**
Metering mode:	**Matrix**
Exposure mode:	**Aperture-priority**
Shutter speed:	**1/200**
Lens aperture:	**F/5.6**

Action
and reaction

For every action there is a reaction … so science says. The question in wildlife photography is whether one can keep pace with the other.

For every action there is a reaction … so science says. The question in wildlife photography is whether one can keep pace with the other. Capturing action shots of animals requires a level of anticipation - of knowing what the subject is about to do rather than pondering on what it has just done. All the following images required a degree of knowledge of animal behaviour to make them happen, recognising the situation and having the camera in the right place at the right time in preparation of unfolding events. Sounds good, I know. Of course occasionally you just happen to get lucky, as I did with the image of the leaping wildebeest. In the trade we call these grab shots, instinctive reactions to an event. Sometimes they come off sometimes they don't, but one thing I can guarantee, the harder you work at getting to know your camera, the luckier you'll get.

African lion,
Greater Kruger National Park, South Africa
All the power and might of a hunting lion is apparent in this all-action shot.

◀ IN THE BAG

Camera:	**D2H**
Lens:	**24-120mm f/3.5-5.6 AF-S VR**
Focal length:	**65mm**
Metering mode:	**Matrix**
Exposure mode:	**Aperture-priority auto**
Shutter speed:	**1/250**
Lens aperture:	**F/11**

Puma, Minnesota, USA
A short focal length lens has created an unusual image of this puma mid-leap. Although the animal fills the frame the wide angle of view helps to maintain a sense of place.

IN THE BAG ▲

Camera:	**D2H**
Lens:	**24-120mm f/3.5-5.6 AF-S VR**
Focal length:	**45mm**
Metering mode:	**Matrix**
Exposure mode:	**Shutter-priority auto**
Shutter speed:	**1/1000**
Lens aperture:	**F/11**
Flash:	**SB-800 Speedlight**

Brown bears, Katmai National Park, Alaska, USA
Territorial disputes are common among bears although rarely result in any real harm to either combatant. In this scene a mother (left) discourages a young interloper.

◄ IN THE BAG

Camera:	**D2X**
Lens:	**600mm f/4 AF**
Focal length:	**600mm**
Metering mode:	**Matrix**
Exposure mode:	**Aperture-priority auto**
Shutter speed:	**1/40**
Lens aperture:	**F/8**

Wildebeeste, Serengeti National Park, Tanzania
For all the planning and research there are times when events simply take over and you either grab the shot, or not. On this occassion I got lucky!

▲ IN THE BAG

Camera:	**D2X**
Lens:	**70-200mm f/2.8 AF-S VR**
Focal length:	**200mm**
Metering mode:	**Matrix**
Exposure mode:	**Aperture-priority auto**
Shutter speed:	**1/1600**
Lens aperture:	**F/8**

Lappet-faced vulture, Kruger National Park, South Africa
As vultures fed on the kill, newcomers would regularly arrive, like planes at an airport. After studying the birds' behaviour I was able to position myself for this classic shot.

IN THE BAG ►

Camera:	**D2X**
Lens:	**80-400mm f/4.5-5.6 AF VR**
Focal length:	**210mm**
Metering mode:	**Matrix**
Exposure mode:	**Aperture-priority auto**
Shutter speed:	**1/640**
Lens aperture:	**F/8**

Face to face

Whether its a stand-off confrontation, hopeless adoration or a mother's love for a baby, photography captures the intimacy of the moment as no other medium can.

Wildlife photography need not always be about capturing rapid action. When I was photographing orang utan in Borneo early in 2006 I spent an entire day concentrating on snapping the facial expressions of the various individuals in the forest. All animals have interesting faces. I admit that some are ugly, while others lend themselves more to good portraiture than others. However, look closely and study animals and you will notice how each has a distinctive characteristic all their own. I mention portraiture because the skills and techniques needed to capture compelling wildlife portraits are much the same as any portrait photographer would adopt and exploit. The following series of images are examples of photographing wildlife face to face.

Brown bears, Katmai National Park, Alaska, USA

As the youngest in the family this yearling brown bear must fight for attention … or even just to get a look in.

◀ **IN THE BAG**

Camera:	**D2X**
Lens:	**80-400mm f/4.5-5.6 AF VR**
Focal length:	**210mm**
Metering mode:	**Matrix**
Exposure mode:	**Aperture-priority auto**
Shutter speed:	**1/400**
Lens aperture:	**F/8**

White rhinoceros, Greater Kruger National Park, South Africa

IN THE BAG ▶

Camera:	**D200**
Lens:	**70-200mm f/2.8 AF-S VR**
Focal length:	**200mm**
Metering mode:	**Matrix**
Exposure mode:	**Aperture-priority**
Shutter speed:	**1/45**
Lens aperture:	**F/4**

Orang utan, Sabah, Borneo

IN THE BAG ▶

Camera:	**D2X**
Lens:	**200-400mm f/4 AF-S VR**
Focal length:	**400mm**
Metering mode:	**Matrix**
Exposure mode:	**Aperture-priority**
Shutter speed:	**1/45**
Lens aperture:	**F/4**

Face to face

Burchell's zebra, Serengeti National Park, Tanzania

Zebras typically drink together, preferring safety in numbers. It's a fine line between serenity and mayhem, however, and the tranquil scene can quickly change, as the converse image on page 41 shows.

IN THE BAG ▶

Camera:	**D2X**
Lens:	**70-200mm f/2.8 AF-S VR with TC 20-E**
Focal length:	**400mm**
Metering mode:	**Matrix**
Exposure mode:	**Aperture-priority auto**
Shutter speed:	**1/1000**
Lens aperture:	**F/7.1**

Face to face

Mountain gorilla, Parc National des Volcanes, Rwanda

Like orang utan gorillas have expressive mannerisms and faces that closely resemble our own. Here a sub-adult male gorilla contemplates life.

IN THE BAG ▶

Camera:	**D200**
Lens:	**70-200mm f/2.8 AF-S VR**
Focal length:	**70mm**
Metering mode:	**Matrix**
Exposure mode:	**Aperture-priority**
Shutter speed:	**1/160**
Lens aperture:	**F/2.8**

Perspective

As a photographer you have the power to reveal the world in many and varied ways.

With little variation human beings see the same way. We stand at roughly the same height and use two eyes to view our surroundings. What that means is that one person's physical view of the world is much the same as another's. If you photograph a subject always from a human standpoint then what the viewer sees is nothing more than they expect. By altering visual perspective you have the ability to jar the viewer, to drag them from their comfort zone and manifest the natural world in such a way that it piques interest and astounds. In so doing your images rise above mediocrity and stand out from the ever-increasing crowd. In the song "Brothers in Arms" by Dire Straits, Mark Knopfler sings "There is just one world but we live in different ones". How we see the world is formed by our life experiences, our emotions and our prejudices, our passions and our preconceptions. No two people see the world the same way. Photography is your means of communicating how the world appears to you.

Perspective

Burchell's zebra, Kruger National Park, South Africa
This image took three years to take. I held the idea in my mind during several trips to Africa but never had the right set of circumstances (quality of light, congregation of animals, location, etc.) fallen into place. Finally an encounter with a herd of 500 zebras in Kruger Park presented the opportunity I'd been waiting for. The subject of this image isn't zebra, it's all about camouflage.

IN THE BAG ▶

Camera:	**D200**
Lens:	**600mm f/4 AF**
Focal length:	**600mm**
Metering mode:	**Matrix**
Exposure mode:	**Aperture-priority**
Shutter speed:	**1/1000**
Lens aperture:	**F/5.6**

Whistling ducks and African elephant, Chobe National Park, Botswana
How you compose an image will also affect how it is perceived. For example, what is the subject of this picture? Is it the ducks in sharp focus in the foreground? Or is it the elephant in the background? Actually, it's neither. The subject of this photograph is size and relativity because what it actually reveals is the gigantic nature of pachyderms.

IN THE BAG ▲

Camera:	**D100**
Lens:	**600mm f/4 AF**
Focal length:	**600mm**
Metering mode:	**Matrix**
Exposure mode:	**Aperture-priority auto**
Shutter speed:	**1/640**
Lens aperture:	**F/8**

Perspective

Giraffe, Kruger National Park, South Africa
This image was taken while I was leading a photo-safari to Kruger Park, and was used to illustrate a point I had made about learning to visualise a subject beyond literal interpretation.

◄ IN THE BAG

Camera:	**D200**
Lens:	**70-200mm f/2.8 AF-S VR**
Focal length:	**200mm**
Metering mode:	**Matrix**
Exposure mode:	**Aperture-priority**
Shutter speed:	**1/250**
Lens aperture:	**F/4**

Focal length
and perspective

Choice of lens focal length will determine the subject's relationship with its environment.

Perspective can be managed via a number of means, not least of which is the focal length of the lens. A wide-angle lens enhances the impression of space and helps to create a sense of place. Features of an animal can be emphasised by this stretching of spacial relationships. Consider the image of a rhinoceros on page 94. An extreme wide-angle lens visually has separated the head from the rest of the body, accentuating the animal's most prominent feature - the horn.

Conversely, a telephoto lens will compress space, making disparate subjects appear closer together. This can be seen in the image of zebras in the Ngorongoro Crater on page 95. The composition has been carefully planned to reveal the animals in proportion to their surroundings. A long focal length lens exaggerates the compositional properties by flattening the scene, reducing any sense of space. Despite appearances, the zebras are around one mile from the crater wall.

Focal length and perspective

White rhinoceros, Masai Mara National Reserve, Kenya

IN THE BAG ▶

Camera:	**D2X**
Lens:	**24-120mm f/3.5-5.6 AF-S VR**
Focal length:	**32mm**
Metering mode:	**Matrix**
Exposure mode:	**Aperture-priority auto**
Shutter speed:	**1/160**
Lens aperture:	**F/8**

Burchell's Zebra, Ngorongoro Crater, Tanzania

IN THE BAG ▶

Camera:	**D2X**
Lens:	**70-200mm f/2.8 AF-S VR**
Focal length:	**190mm**
Metering mode:	**Matrix**
Exposure mode:	**Aperture-priority auto**
Shutter speed:	**1/800**
Lens aperture:	**F/8**

Focal length and perspective

Griffon vulture, Haut Provence, France

IN THE BAG ▶

Camera:	**D2H**
Lens:	**24-120mm f/3.5-5.6 AF-S VR**
Focal length:	**120mm**
Metering mode:	**Matrix**
Exposure mode:	**Aperture-priority auto**
Shutter speed:	**1/2000**
Lens aperture:	**F/5.6**

Nile crocodile, Limpopo, South Africa

Lenses affect spacial relationships, altering the manner in which individual pictorial elements within the frame interact. For example, for the image of the crocodile, above, I used a wide-angle lens to emphasise the dangerous end of the reptile. By stretching the spacial relationship between foreground, middle-ground and background, the crocodile's jaws become pre-eminent, while the image retains a sense of place avoiding the possibility of the image becoming abstract in its nature.

▲ IN THE BAG

Camera:	**D2H**
Lens:	**12-24mm f/4 AF-S DX**
Focal length:	**24mm**
Metering mode:	**Matrix**
Exposure mode:	**Aperture-priority auto**
Shutter speed:	**1/350**
Lens aperture:	**F/8**

African elephant, Chobe National Park, Botswana

◄ IN THE BAG

Camera:	**D2X**
Lens:	**70-200mm f/2.8 AF-S VR**
Focal length:	**78mm**
Metering mode:	**Matrix**
Exposure mode:	**Aperture-priority**
Shutter speed:	**1/400**
Lens aperture:	**F/8**

African elephant, Greater Kruger National Park, South Africa

Ever wondered how the world appears to an elephant? An unusual angle and an extreme focal length combine to create an evocative and contrasting image.

IN THE BAG ►

Camera:	**D2H**
Lens:	**12-24mm f/4 AF-S DX**
Focal length:	**12mm**
Metering mode:	**Matrix**
Exposure mode:	**Aperture-priority auto**
Shutter speed:	**1/500**
Lens aperture:	**F/11**

Flamingos,
Parc National Regional de Camargue, France
By squashing spacial relationships this flock of flamingos appears more tightly bunched than they actually were, increasing the sense of numbers that the scene demanded.

◀ IN THE BAG

Camera:	**D2H**
Lens:	**80–400mm f/4.5–5.6 AF VR**
Focal length:	**220mm**
Metering mode:	**Matrix**
Exposure mode:	**Aperture-priority auto**
Shutter speed:	**1/350**
Lens aperture:	**F/8**

Flamingos, Ngorongoro Crater, Tanzania
Despite the fact these birds were quite separated the use of a long telephoto lens has brought them apparently together, giving extra weight to the numbers and making the visual perception closer to the sense of reality.

IN THE BAG ▶

Camera:	**D!00**
Lens:	**600mm f/4 AF**
Focal length:	**600mm**
Metering mode:	**Matrix**
Exposure mode:	**Aperture-priority auto**
Shutter speed:	**1/350**
Lens aperture:	**F/16**

Eye **to eye**

The angle from which we photograph wildlife greatly affects our relationship with the subject.

The visual relationship we share with the subject is at its most powerful when we are on the same psychological plane, i.e. when we are at eye level. Frequently this means obeying my first law of wildlife photography … you don't get to go home until you're dirty!

Next time you're out photographing try the angle theory for yourself, if the subject allows. Photograph an animal from above, from below and at eye level and study how the psychological impacts of the comparative images vary.

In the meantime, think about how your visual relationship with the lion in the picture on *page 109* would alter had I shot it from above. Of course, there is an exception to every rule. The photograph of the crocodile (page 103) was purposely shot from above because I wanted to emphasise the animal's profile.

Nile crocodile, Limpopo, South Africa

IN THE BAG ▶

Camera:	**D100**
Lens:	**80-400mm f/4.5-5.6 AF VR**
Focal length:	**400mm**
Metering mode:	**Matrix**
Exposure mode:	**Aperture-priority auto**
Shutter speed:	**1/250**
Lens aperture:	**F/11**

Brown bear, Katmai National Park, Alaska, USA
A combination of camera angle (eye level) and spacial relationship (squashed) has emphasised the behaviour of this bear, which is snuffling for clams on the Katmai Peninsular.

◄ IN THE BAG

Camera:	**D2X**
Lens:	**600mm f/4 AF**
Focal length:	**600mm**
Metering mode:	**Matrix**
Exposure mode:	**Aperture-priority auto**
Shutter speed:	**1/80**
Lens aperture:	**F/8**

Cheetahs, Ngorongoro Crater, Tanzania
Photographing wildlife with the camera postioned at eye level relative to the subject will generally enhance the power of the image, putting subject and photographer on an equal footing.

IN THE BAG ▲

Camera:	**D2X**
Lens:	**80-400MM F/4.5-5.6 AF VR**
Focal length:	**400mm**
Metering mode:	**Matrix**
Exposure mode:	**Aperture-priority auto**
Shutter speed:	**1/500**
Lens aperture:	**F/11**

African lionesses, Masai Mara National Reserve, Kenya

◄ IN THE BAG

Camera:	**D2X**
Lens:	**600mm f/4 AF**
Focal length:	**600mm**
Metering mode:	**Matrix**
Exposure mode:	**Aperture-priority auto**
Shutter speed:	**1/500**
Lens aperture:	**F/8**

Grey wolf, Minnesota, USA

The psychological impact of this image is made stronger by the low camera angle, which gives an eye level view of the subject.

IN THE BAG ►

Camera:	**D2H**
Lens:	**70-200mm f/2.8 AF-S VR**
Focal length:	**120mm**
Metering mode:	**Matrix**
Exposure mode:	**Aperture-priority auto**
Shutter speed:	**1/1250**
Lens aperture:	**F/8**

**African elephant calf,
Kruger National Park, South Africa**
By excluding all but a small section of adult elephant
context is given to the calf sheltering behind the safety of
the adults' legs.

◄ IN THE BAG

Camera:	**D2X**
Lens:	**70-200mm f/2.8 AF-S VR**
Focal length:	**200mm**
Metering mode:	**Matrix**
Exposure mode:	**Aperture-priority auto**
Shutter speed:	**1/320**
Lens aperture:	**F/8**

African lion,
Greater Kruger National Park, South Africa
Our relationship to a subject is determined by the angle at which it's photographed. In human terms we call it the parent/child relationship. When we look down at something or someone we assume superiority. The opposite occurs when we look up. Parents look down at children and our greater knowledge and experience places us in superiority. Children look up at parents and feel subordinate to them (although as a relatively new parent I'm beginning to question this particular observation).

◀ IN THE BAG

Camera:	**D2H**
Lens:	**24-120mm f/3.5-5.6 AF-S VR**
Focal length:	**70mm**
Metering mode:	**Matrix**
Exposure mode:	**Aperture-priority auto**
Shutter speed:	**1/750**
Lens aperture:	**F/5.6**

Equipment

I was first introduced to Nikon cameras in 1977 when my father gave me as a present his old Nikkormat FT 35mm film camera, which he had purchased while stationed with the RAF in Singapore in the early '60's. I used that camera for several years, shunning such technological advances as auto-focus and increasingly sophisticated TTL-meters - although truth be told I secretly coveted the much heralded, then top-of-the-range F3.

It was fifteen years before I succumbed, when in 1992 I bought a brand new F90X for the princely sum of £900. The F90X is, in my mind, a superb camera and it served me well for six years until, in 1998, I decided to turn my love of photography from a hobby into a career. I upgraded to the F5 and continued with that as my main camera until 2003 when I unwittingly passed to the 'other side'.

The genesis of my conversion was, in all honesty, whimsical. I had a system of medium format gear that I wanted to get rid of but couldn't think of anything I needed in part exchange. With a sudden rush of blood to the head I decided to try out digital (about which, until then, I had been determinedly sceptical) and I traded my 6x7 body and five lenses for a D100, thinking I would try it out in my few moments of spare time. I took it on a field trip to Africa shortly after acquiring it and at the end of the first day I decided to give it a go. From that moment, I rarely put it down. Since then the F5 and F90X have gone to be replaced by a D2H (now also departed), a D2X and two D200 bodies. Yes, my name is Chris and I'm a digital convert.

What is interesting about this potted history is that throughout the nearly thirty years I have been using Nikon cameras I have never felt uncomfortable with a Nikon camera in my hand. They are, for me, a camera designed by photographers for photographers, and while other manufacturers may do things quicker, rarely I find have they ever managed to do them better.

The D2X and two D200s now form the mainstay of my professional work and, after five cameras in three years, I hope they will continue to do so for some time to come. But despite my reliance on new technology, if you look hard into the dusty corner of my studio you will find an old Nikkormat FT and a slightly younger F3. Yes, I eventually picked one up on E-bay!

Cheetahs and Burch ell's zebra, Ngorongoro Crater, Tanzania

While it is true to say that the camera is less important than the photographer, sometimes equipment enables us to achieve things that would otherwise be close to impossible. This image is a composite of two RAW files overlayed in camera using a function on the D2X camera. The first image taken was of the zebra in the background, with the focus point on the middle zebra. I then shot a second, separate image of the cheetahs, which were laying slightly to the left of and at a right angle to the zebras. I then overlayed the images in-camera to produce this interesting and effective result.

IN THE BAG ▶

Camera:	**D2X**
Lens:	**200-400mm f/4 AF-S VR**
Focal length:	**280mm**
Metering mode:	**Matrix**
Exposure mode:	**Aperture-priority auto**
Shutter speed:	**1/750**
Lens aperture:	**F/11**

The following table is a list of the Nikon equipment used in the making of this book.

F90X 35mm film camera
F5 35mm film camera
D100 digital camera with MB-D100
D2H digital camera
D2X digital camera
D200 digital camera with MB-D200

12-24mm f/4 AF-S DX zoom lens
24-120mm f/3.5-5.6 AF VR zoom lens
24-120mm f/3.5-5.6 AF zoom lens
80-200mm f/2.8 AF zoom lens
70-200mm f/2.8 AF-S VR zoom lens
300mm f/2.8 AF prime lens
80-400mm f/4.5-5.6 AF VR zoom lens
200-400mm f/4 AF-S VR zoom lens
600mm f/4 AF prime lens
TC - 20E tele-converter

SB-800 Speedlight
SC-29 flash extension cord

MC20 remote shutter release
MC-21 remote shutter release extension cord
ML-3 infrared remote control

Type EC-E focusing screen
L37c filters

Coolscan IV ED 35mm film scanner
Nikon View v.6 digital workflow software
Capture 4.2 Editor digital workflow software
Capture 4.2 Camera Control software

Appendix

Useful contacts

At the heart of the image

Nikon Corporation
Head Office
Fuji Building
2-3 Marunouchi 3-chome
Chiyoda-ku
Tokyo
100-8331
Japan
Tel: +81 3 3214 5311
Web: www.nikon.com

Nikon Photo Products Inc.
23-1 Azumabashi 1-chome
Sumida-ku
Tokyo
130-8677
Japan
Tel: +81 3 5608 5500

Nikon UK Ltd
380 Richmond Road
Kingston upon Thames
Surrey
KT2 5PR
UK
Tel: +44 (0) 20 8541 4440

Nikon Inc.
1300 Walt Whitman Road
Melville
New York
11747-3064
USA
Tel: +1 631 547 4200

Nikon Canada Inc.
1366 Aerowood Drive
Mississauga
Ontario
L4W 1C1
Canada
Tel: +1 905 625 9910

Nikon Europe B.V.
New Yorkstraat 66
1175 RD Lijnden
The Netherlands
Tel: +31 20 4496 222

Nikon GmbH
Tiefenbroicher Weg 25
40472 Dusseldorf
Germany
Tel: +49 211 94 140

Nikon France S.A.S.
191 rue du Marché Rollay
94504 Champigny sur Marne
Cedex
France
Tel: +33 1 45 16 45 16

Nikon Nordic AB
Anton Tamms väg 3
Box 84
194 22 Upplands-Väsby
Sweden
Tel: +46 8 594 109 00

Chris Weston

Natural Photographic Ltd
2nd Floor Studios
3 Roman Road
Weymouth
Dorset
DT3 5JQ
UK
Tel: +44 (0) 1305 770264
Web: www.chrisweston.uk.com

Grays of Westminster

40 Churton Street
Pimlico
London
SW1V 2LP
UK
Tel: +44 (0) 20 7828 4925
Web: www.graysofwestminster.co.uk

Nikon Owner

40 Churton Street
Pimlico
London
SW1V 2LP
UK
Tel: +44 (0) 20 7592 9282
Web: www.nikonownermagazine.com

Appendix

Useful websites

Nikonians - worldwide community for Nikon users

www.nikonians.org

dpreview: Nikon general forum

http://forums.dpreview.com/forums/forum.asp?forum=1007

dpreview: Nikon D50/D70 forum

http://forums.dpreview.com/forums/forum.asp?forum=1034

dpreview: Nikon D1/D2/D100/D200 forum

http://forums.dpreview.com/forums/forum.asp?forum=1021

dpreview: Nikon SLR lens forum

http://forums.dpreview.com/forums/forum.asp?forum=1030

dpreview: Nikon camera reviews

www.dpreview.com/reviews/specs/Nikon/